The Art of Flipping Art

Buying & Selling Art
For Huge Profits

By Rick Cheadle

The Art Of Flipping Art

Copyright 2015 by Rick Cheadle

Legal Disclaimer

This book contains strategies and tips and other business advice that, regardless of my own experiences and results, may not produce the same results for you. You understand that I make no guarantees regarding income as a result of applying this information, as well as the fact that you are responsible for the results of any action taken on your part as a result of the information provided in this book.

Dear reader,

Thank you for purchasing my book. "The Art of Flipping Art: Buying and Selling Art for Huge Profits" . This book outlines the proven steps I take when buying and selling art as part of my thrifting and reselling business.

Fine art is an $80 billion global market. The fine art market is a fun, profitable and often overlooked segment of the "flipping" community. Art comes in many forms - paintings, sculptures, vintage jewelry, objects, silverware, ceramics, antique furniture, etc.

The topics covered in this book will be for wall art; oil paintings, watercolors, lithographs etc. and bronze sculptures.

There are tens of thousands of dollars out there waiting to be made if you know how to do it. I will share with you how I have profited tens of thousands of dollars buying and selling art part time with no formal training and no art buying background. Throughout this book I will share with you my art buying and selling stories good and bad.

You will be able to learn what to do and more importantly what NOT to do. In this book I'm going to provide you with the resources that you'll need to find incredible deals and sell them for the highest possible profit.

By following the techniques outlined in this book, you will have enough knowledge to start making money immediately only investing a few hours per week. Are you ready?

Great!

To Your Success!

Rick Cheadle

Table of Contents

Introduction

Flipping art is a serious business just like any other. The biggest mistake I see people make over and over again is thinking that they're going to make a series of long shots and soon "hit the lottery". This mentality will not work in the art flipping world.

Too often we don't consider the worst case scenario of a particular investment until we've put all our money down. If you want to realize any profit, you must see the bigger picture.

That's why becoming an expert is vital to your success. The fact that you need to come to terms with is that there are people just like you who've turned a vague interest in art into a profitable hobby. It is a possibility for people who are serious.

I've actually turned it into a full time career with a full time income to support myself and my family. If I can do it, you can too.

The tools and resources are all laid out for you. The fact that you've invested in this book tells me that you're ready to pull the trigger, or at least find out what really goes on inside the world of art flipping. But you must be committed to learning everything that you can before you can move forward on this journey.

You must be willing to do whatever it takes to achieve success. More often than not, the actual techniques used in flipping art are simple and easy to use, but there are some important things you need to know, that make it all work. I'm going to reveal them to you in this book.

You may have heard the phrase "do the right things long enough consistently". As you know, nobody can guarantee your success in this field, but the methods revealed in this book will work for you if you apply them correctly. That's my promise.

Flipping art is an incredibly fun way of making money. If you're with me so far, then you're ready for me to peel back the curtain and reveal the secrets of successfully flipping art for huge profits. Let's move forward, shall we?

Chapter 1

How much money can you make buying and selling art?

These are a few examples of some of the art I have bought and sold over the past few years:

Adolph Gottlieb c.1949 gouache, watercolor, ink on paper

Bought for **$24** at Estate Auction

Sold for **$29,000** one month later

This piece now resides at Michael Rosenfeld Gallery in NYC

Yes that's me!

Paul Jenkins "Phenomena, Jade Winds Walking"

Bought for **$57** at a Repossession Sale

Sold for **$23,000** two months later at Major Auction House

This canvas was so large I had to rent a U Haul to transport it! Here is a picture of it in my dining room.

Gene Davis Silkscreen "King Kong"

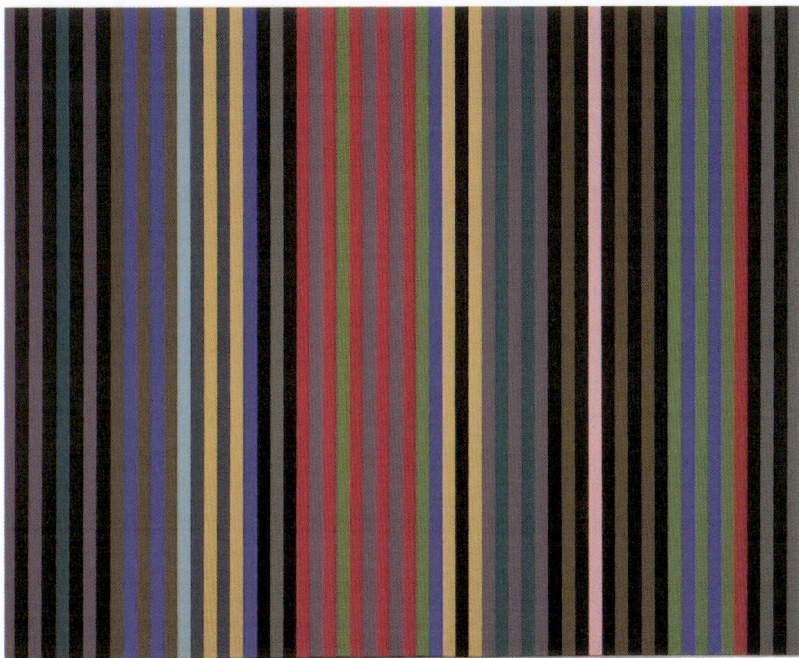

Bought for **$30** at an estate sale

Sold for **$850** on E Bay two weeks later

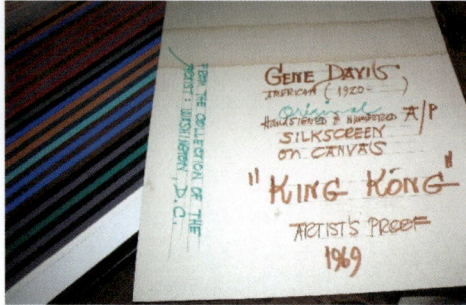

The board pictured on the right side of this photo with all of the writing was hidden behind the backing cover, that is why you must take the cover off to see what lies beneath!

Salvador Dali "Intra-Uterine Paradisiac Locomotion"

Bought for **$33** on online estate auction

Sold for **$750** at local Art Gallery three weeks later

Doing your homework pays off. No one at the auction
(including the auctioneer) knew what this was but I did!

Hy Golo "Girl"

Bought for **$5** at a frame shop

Sold for **$350** to a private collector

Hy Golo "Sinatra"

Bought for **$5** at a frame shop

Sold for **$250** to a private collector

You want the reality, right? Well, I promised I would share the good and the bad, and I'm not going to hold anything back. You must understand the risks.

After my first couple experiences with buying and selling art I was hooked! I was eager to find more paintings and repeat the process. I started to think, "Man this is easy. I just have to buy a high quality painting, take it to an auction house and make money!"

In theory that is true. BUT I was careless and I let my ego and naivety get the best of me and I quickly learned an expensive lesson. In short, it is this: Consider the Source. Here's how I learned (the hard way) how to get ALL the facts before buying a piece of art. Here's the story.

I was researching an online art auction that was coming up and I came across a unique looking painting with a name I had recently read about. The artist was *Francis Picabia*.

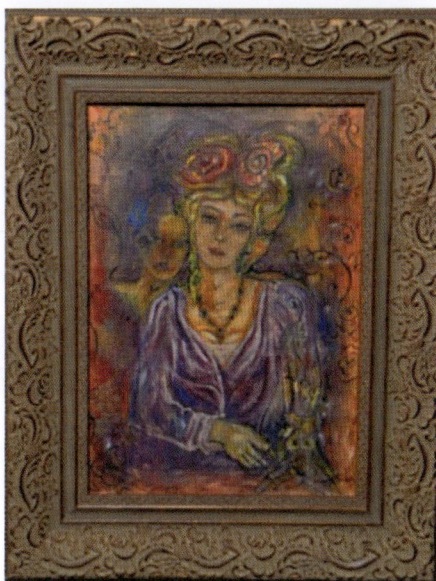

signed Francis Picabia oil on canvas

Some of his auction records for his recently sold paintings were in the $50,000 range and this particular painting only had a pre-auction estimate of $3,000 - $4,000. I thought, "Wow this could be something". So I did more research and studied the signature as best as I could. It looked legit.

There was a bill of sale in the listing that was in a foreign language but I thought "it's got to be legit". I was thinking, "The auction house don't realize what they have here. I gotta get this one!"

Well it turns out they did know what they had. A painting that was signed with the name Francis Picabia. That's it.

No provenance no authentication, nothing but a painting with a signature. Later I realized that explained the low pre-auction estimate.

The auction house didn't mislead me. The auction title was "signed Francis Picabia oil on canvas" and that is exactly what it was. This mistake was totally on me.

I paid $1700 for this piece and I thought I got a steal. I was gonna flip this and make $40,000 - $50,000 right?

Wrong: It turns out the signature was a forgery and it could not be authenticated. I was stunned.

Signature forgeries are an all too common occurrence in the world of art. I didn't know that at the time and it cost me. I had to reevaluate everything. I knew it wasn't going to be as easy as I thought in the future.   I knew had had to do my homework. I knew I had to start using my head when making buying decisions and not allow myself to get emotionally invested in any future art purchases.

Please. Learn from my mistake. You can't wish a painting to be something special. It either is or it's not. You MUST do your homework and keep your emotions out of the equation. I ended up selling the painting for $500. So that turned out to be a $1200 lesson learned.

Chapter 2

Getting Started

Immerse Yourself in the Art World

The only way to know what the water's like is to get full immersion. Dipping your toe and casually observing buyers, sellers and various pieces will not bring comprehension. Remember this critical point.

You can develop a 'sense' for the market. To better understand why there is such a high demand for art and why people are willing to pay so much money for it, you should try to gain all the knowledge you can on the subject of art. It's not as complicated as it may seem.

But you must have a working knowledge base. I'm not saying you have to study art history or have a degree or anything, just get involved with and be around art. There's a few simple ways to do that.

Strategy # 1

Research online

Familiarize yourself with basics of art. What styles, colors or subjects are popular? Is black and white photography popular? What about modern abstract paintings or still lifes? A simple Google search can tell you this.

Explore and observe what is out there. You'll build more

confidence each day, and you'll start to feel the momentum. There is an infinite amount of knowledge to be found on the web.

Strategy #2

Attend an art auction

Don't be intimidated. You can usually find a fine art auction in any major city. You don't have to bid on anything or even show up with money in your pocket. The key is just being there, taking it all in.

That may not be possible for you right now. If attending a fine art auction is not an option another strategy to use is to find art auctions that are hosted online. You will be able to hear the auctioneer and visually follow along on your computer screen "live".

The key is to gain first-hand experience. Once you begin to see how the whole process works and get familiar with the various art related terms and descriptions used, you'll have a great deal of artistic comprehension. You'll also become more familiar with the types, styles, schools and eras of art that exist. This is exactly the information you want in order to make money in art.

Strategy #3

Local Galleries and Museums

There are two classifications: Exclusive and Open public.

Exclusive galleries are operated for private purposes of promoting and selling artworks.

An open public gallery is generally called a museum. It displays works of art from renowned artists and makes them available for public viewing either temporarily or permanently.

Try to find galleries or museums that show art from pre 1980. Although there are modern and contemporary artists that command high prices for their work, the work is very subjective and there isn't a lot on the market to purchase inexpensively. That is the key in making money in art.

Flipping 101 Buy low, sell high. Make sure to ask questions and take the tours they have available. Absorb all the knowledge you can. Watch other visitors to see what art they like. These things will serve you well in the future.

Strategy #4

Old Art Books

Your local library or used bookstores are both good places to find art books. You can find a particular era of art or style to focus on or general art collecting. These books contain a wealth of information that you want to have in your pocket. Very helpful tool.

Strategy #5

Auction Catalogs

Try to find auction catalogs from major auction houses. You will also want to download the "Prices Realized" sheet so you can use for future reference and research.

Another tip would be to make sure the catalog is post 2008. The market crash affected the art market just like everything else. You want the most up to date and relevant auction prices to refer to when determining the current value of art

Strategy #6

Find a Mentor

There are many people in the art world. Some are a wealth of valuable information and are more than willing to share their knowledge and experiences. Seek them out and absorb like a sponge.

Observe how they act. Their habits and wisdom will rub off on you, and you'll gain tremendous insight and perspective. Take their counsel and opinions. Often being able to see things through other people's eyes will help you predict future trends. Their advice can be invaluable.

This concludes getting started. In this chapter I focused on helping you build a general understanding of the art world, and the many facets you can get involved with. You must build this foundation before moving ahead.

I can tell you that these are the steps you must take first. It can seem a bit overwhelming but if you gradually ease into it you will feel more and more confident. You will start to know the ins and outs.

When you can recognize the hot trends and discern where the market is heading in the future, you can potentially make a lot of money. These are important factors because when buying and selling art knowledge is power.

Chapter 3

How the Art Business Works and the Key Players

Galleries

The main role of art galleries is to promote and sell fine art. Don't underestimate this opportunity to discover the nature of your prospective buyers, as well as the art that they're looking for. Here's how it works.

Art lovers visit art galleries and examine the exhibited art pieces. If the artwork is good, it will gain recognition and the artist may become well known. There are two terms you should become well aware of.

Art galleries sell at "retail" prices. Many times you will hear appraisers quote "retail estimates" of an item. That is a gallery retail price they are referring to. On the other hand "auction estimates" tend to be lower.

Art Dealers

These are people you want to acquaint yourself with. An art dealer basically represents artists and builds relationships with collectors and galleries who may be interested in an artist's work. But you need to be aware of something here.

When dealers buy works of art, they resell them either in their galleries or directly to collectors. What you want to keep in mind is that most gallery owners are also dealers but not all dealers are gallery owners.

This is important to know before approaching galleries for advice.

Art Brokers

Art brokers connect buyers with sellers for a commission. An art brokers can also be hired by wealthy consumers to purchase art for them so their identity can remain anonymous.

Pickers

A picker is the person who does the leg work. They go to estate sale, flea markets, garage sales and yes even go dumpster diving. Once the picker finds something of value, they will usually sell it to a dealer or gallery.

Investors

Art as an investment is gaining popularity. Because of the demand and market trends, many new buyers have arrived and are willing to spend their hard earned money on a prospective piece.

Get to know them and what they're looking for. Investors are a good source to try to sell a valuable piece of art if you can speak their language. Thinking long term with them will help tremendously.

Collectors

These are your most desirable clients. Your goal should be to try to find a collector to purchase your piece of art because they will pay much more than a gallery, dealer or investor. They are basically "end game".

The piece of art will end up on their wall. Finding collectors for a particular piece is a hard prospect. It can be done but it take a lot of leg work.

Auction Houses

Auction houses deal with many types of people. They see private collectors, pickers, dealers, pretty much anyone who has a piece of art that has value that they can make a profit on.

Auction houses are also good for you. You can bring them the art you find in order to gauge how well you are doing finding quality pieces of art to resell. Let me explain.

They're a valid indicator of market value. If they are a legitimate auction house and they are willing to sell your piece of art for you, they believe it is authentic. They can offer a lot of clarity this way.

It's a basic sign that you are on the right track in your art reselling venture!

Museums

Museums rarely if ever purchase are from people off the street. They deal with auction houses and dealers with an established reputation, and don't have time for people that don't have that kind of credibility. However, you should know who they are and what they do.

Art Appraisers

An art appraiser can identify your pieces. By examining artwork themselves they can determine whether or not it's authentic. An art appraiser also determines the fair market value of paintings.

Insurers

Protect your art from theft or the elements. If you have a valuable piece of art, get it appraised and get it insured for twice the appraisal amount. The reasons are obvious.

Just make sure you take the time to do this. Sometimes we're so eager thinking about our brand new TV or something silly like that, that we forget this is a business. Be intelligent whenever you take financial risk.

Chapter 4
Where to Find Valuable Art

Get in the habit of always looking. Any place you go and anywhere you are, keep your eyes open. You never know where the next big score is hiding. (The Adolph Gottlieb gouache on paper piece is something I found hiding on a dirty floor between two mirrors)

This is where your dedication to research will come into play. Keep in mind that when the rubber hits the road, it's just as important as ever to stay consistent in practicing the methods taught in this book on a daily regular basis.

What differentiates this from picking up trash on the side of the road and selling it on eBay, is expertise. The following are some very promising places to find unclaimed, high quality art.

Garage Sales/Yard Sales

This is our first area of untold riches. When most people hold garage or yard sales their goal is to get rid of a bunch of stuff that they see as junk. They're usually satisfied to unclutter their house for a small amount of money.

Here's what you need to know. Most people who have these sales will not know about the true value of all of the items they are selling. This presents a great opportunity for you to find some hidden gems.

I have found original framed oil paintings and lithographs for as little as $1 at these sales!

Estate/Tag Sales

About half of estate sales are held when someone dies. The other half occur when a homeowner decides to downsize to a smaller home for example following a divorce or retirement.

Because the sales are designed to sell off a large portion of a home's contents quickly, you can expect prices to be lower than what one would find at a retail store or antique shop. The key is to research before you go.

Make sure you check out the estate sale company's website for details and photos for potential treasures. If you decide to go, I recommend getting there early. Most of the "good stuff" sells within the first few hours but there are exceptions.

Craigslist

Go to craigslist.org and find the city nearest you. Press the "for sale" tab then in the search box try these different search terms:

- painting
- watercolor oil painting
- picture

You can try this in all of the cities you'd like. It is time consuming but it could pay off, like when I found a couple of really nice Bernard Buffet Lithographs. I bought them from a guy on Craigslist for $30 and a few weeks later sold them for $225 on Ebay.

Etsy

I have not found anything on Etsy personally but I think it is worth looking in to. Use same search terms as listed under Craigslist

eBay

eBay is one of my favorite sources for finding great deals on art. There are thousands of paintings at your disposal. To make the process a little more manageable I recommend using the advanced search option then do the following:

- In the keywords or item number box type the word "oil"

- then in the *In this category* search box select Art

- under *search including* select Title and description

- then farther down the page go to *Show results* section

- select *Listings* ending within 12 hours,

- and *Number of bids from* enter the number 1 (this means that at least one person bid on this item and it is guaranteed to be sold)

I use this advanced search criteria every time I am sourcing for art on eBay.

Online Auctions

Another good option to find art.

Check here for online auctions www.auctionzip.com

Also another good one to check out is www.shopgoodwill.com

Storage Auctions

You've seen them on TV. They are an option but risky since you can't physically examine the contents before bidding. Use with caution.

Flea Markets/Swap Meets

Excellent sources for vintage art and usually very inexpensive!

Antique Stores

Antique stores can be pricey but they are worth checking out.

Consignment Stores/Thrift Shops

Great places to find treasures for cheap!

Other Ideas

Tell your friends and relatives, make flyers, create business cards, start a website. Let the world know that you buy and sell art.

Chapter 5

How to Authenticate your Art

This step is absolutely essential. Just like everything you've already learned, this will take some research, but over time will become second nature. I've simplified the process for you.

First, there is something you must know before I share the various methods with you.

It comes down to basic negotiation. If you're going to sell your art to somebody, chances are they probably know what they're doing, and you should too. Here's a basic example.

You're speaking to a prospective client, and they ask you to name a price. If you haven't done your homework, this could be a very costly mistake. Here's why.

Number one, any decent negotiator will listen to your asking price and say, "It's not going to happen". This is the easiest way to get low-balled.

The solution is to have solid knowledge of what your art is worth, multiple references, and KNOW first-hand what you're willing to part with it for.

Like we said before, this isn't about making a quick buck, and you want to get paid everything you're worth. Let's now discuss the various ways to do that.

Provenance

The documented ownership history of the piece is valuable

information, and there are many methods used to determine provenance.

Usually, it is shown with a combination of more than one of the following: a signed certificate or statement of authenticity by an expert, an exhibition or gallery sticker, the original sales receipt, or a photo of the artist with the work.

Also, a list of previous owners, letters from experts concerning the art, articles written, picture of the piece in a catalog or brochure, appraisal from a recognized authority, and/or a verbal history from someone familiar with the artist also establishes provenance.

If a piece of art has provenance established, additional analysis is not needed. You can rest assured that you're buying an original.

If there is no established provenance there are other methods to use to authenticate, first of all, that it is an actual painting. You also need to verify whether the artist signature is real or fake.

Is it really a Painting?

Appearances can be deceiving, and I learned that the hard way. What may appear to be an oil painting may in fact be a print or color photograph with some clear acrylic gel. It doesn't end there though.

The brushstrokes can even be misleading. Medium or varnish brushstrokes can be applied to the surface to give it the appearance of a real oil painting. It is easy to be fooled so pay attention.

A REAL PAINTING will have REAL paint brushstrokes Make sure you hold the painting up to the light, and use a magnifying glass or ideally a jewelers loop. Authentic brushstrokes will vary in size, shape and texture.

Now hold your canvas up to the light again. Look from the reverse side of the painting and check to make sure that there are variations in the amount of light coming through. Here's how to spot a fake.

A real painting will have these variations due to the amount of paint used on different areas of the painting surface. A print will not have these variations.

Here's how you can verify a watercolor painting. An original watercolor will have a rough surface when looked at from an angle; a reproduction will have a flat and even surface. Always remember those details.

You should also be able to tell a copy from an original. Lithographs and other multiples hand-made by the artist usually have an artist's signature. They'll also have the number of the work, if part of a series.

For example, 7/75 means the seventh work of a series of seventy five in total. These are considered originals and the signature and numbers are hand-written by the artist. Remember to check for those details as well.

Remove the Backing Cover!

Some paintings have what's referred to as a dust-cover, or backing paper. It is easily and inexpensively replaced in the event that it is torn or removed completely. Removing them is a requirement for all authentications.

Remove the Frame

This can be done without any damage done to the painting and can easily be replaced.

Once the frame is removed examine the edges of the canvas. When an artist paints, there is usually paint that gets on the edges of the canvas, although not always.

Some artists do use tape to get a clean edge, but there should be some seepage under the tape or paint splashes, speckles etc. that you can see.

If it is a print, you will see a straight and very clean line that marks where the art ends. This is made by a machine and more than likely not an original piece of art.

Sometimes fake brushstrokes are added on top of the clean lines. These are actually attempts to scam buyers by concealing the straight line. With careful examination you will see the line clearly beneath.

This is a piece that should be passed on unless you think it's pretty and would look nice hanging on your wall.

Examine Your Painting with a Magnifying Glass or Jeweler's Loupe

Examine the front of the piece. What you are looking for is little dots which are made from a printer. This is immediate evidence that you are not looking at an original piece of art.

Remember these are things to look for when you are out prospecting. Ultimately to determine if you have a winner you should have a certified art appraiser or an auction house inspect each piece as well.

Blacklight Test

Another way of spotting a painting that is not an original is by using a long wave blacklight. If you are examining a painting that has a heavy textured surface and the varnish appears clear just shine a blacklight on the surface and see what happens. If it glows white, it is likely a texturized print. Pass on this.

Is the Artist "Listed"?

A "listed" artist is a term used to describe an artist that has at least one auction record to their name. I prefer to buy art from listed artists with at least 5 auction results so I can get a good idea of what the market is for his or her work

Artist Signature

Research the artist signature at libraries & museums. Read about the artist online, and also in paper-printed books with signature images. These are incredibly valuable tools at validating a signature.

Some of these books include:

Castagno, John, ed. American Artists Signatures and Monograms, 1800-1989. Metuchen, N.J.: Scarecrow Press, 1990.

Falk, Peter Hastings, ed. Dictionary of Signatures and Monograms of American Artists. Madison, CT.: Sound View Press, 1988.

Chapter 6

What's it worth?

Many factors must be considered in determining an artwork's monetary value.

Condition is one of the most important factors in assessing value, followed by provenance and recent auction prices realized for similar works by the same artist.

This information can be found by looking at public sales records. My favorite tool for finding this information is on websites like askart.com or artvalue.com, which are valuable resources for research.

Subject matter is also a factor. Landscapes and still life's sell better then dark and ominous art, which is something you'll discover on your own as well. This may seem like common sense, but just keep the general concept in mind.

Rarity is another essential aspect. It's determined by the frequency with which a work by an artist appears on the market.

Although a paintings value is subject to many variables, these variables are not always relevant.

For example, guidelines for insurance or sales appraisals may be more specific in nature than the definitions described above. A collector might also assign a painting a value based on a more emotional level.

In any case, understanding the background of a painting, the condition and its current market can all be indicators of the paintings current market value.

That being said, there isn't an exact dollar amount that can be given on any piece of art. But you can get a price range.

Past auction results are used for giving an estimate but that is exactly what it is - an estimate.

For example, you may have a piece of art that has a pre-auction estimate of $3,000 - $5,000. Then a bidding war ensues and the final auction price ends up being $10,000.

Conversely, the same time the same piece of art with the same pre-auction estimate may not even receive an opening bid. You just never know.

I personally would avoid paying for an appraiser. You can get a good idea if you have something of value by doing your own research and/or by sending photos of the painting to the major auction houses.

They will respond with estimates and suggestions. I would contact Sotheby's or Christies.

Chapter 7

Where to Sell your Art

Auction Houses

This should be your number one place to sell. I mentioned Christie's and Sotheby's; there is also Phillips, Bonhams and DuMouchelle's . You can google auction houses and find others as well.

Try to sell your piece by consignment. This means that you list your piece with them, and if they sell it, they take a portion of the sale price (commission). I would try to negotiate a lower commission fee.

Some of the auction houses will lower their consignment fee especially if you have a valuable painting that they want to include in their auction. You want to find out every time.

Sometimes an auction house will not want your piece at all. This does happen, and if it does happen to you, ask them if they know of someone else that would be interested.

If they do want your piece, you are on your way to flipping your art!

Dealers and Brokers

Look up dealers that specialize in the artist that created your painting. The easiest way is to Google the "artists name" followed by "dealers" or Google "Where to buy a painting by

_____"? That should give you plenty of avenues to pursue.

Be wary of scam dealers. If they try to make a low-ball offer or ask you to send your art to them for analysis or if your gut just says no, then keep looking.

When discussing the sale of the art at first try not to give a price. Ask them to make you an offer. If you say that you want five thousand for a piece, chances are you won't get it.

If you do have to give a price, start high. You can always negotiate down to the price you wanted in the beginning.

eBay

eBay is a proven place to sell art. Make sure you are very thorough when entering the listing, and include the maximum amount of pictures allowed. Also ensure that your terms of sale are very clear.

In addition, figure out how you are going to charge shipping, and always get insurance. I would also recommend that you have a reserve price so that you don't undersell.

Sculptures

Buying and Selling Sculptures

I'm sure you have a general idea of what a sculpture is. You probably have seen them on TV shows like Antiques Roadshow or at an antique store or you may even own one. There is a wide variety of styles, composition and materials used when artists create sculptures.

By definition a sculpture is basically described as the art of making two or three-dimensional forms by carving stone or wood or by casting metal or plaster. While it is important for you to learn everything that you can about all types of sculptures, the focus in this book for "flipping" purposes will be on bronze sculptures. In particular; authentic, antique bronze sculptures that are in good to excellent condition.

There is good profits to be made in flipping bronze sculptures as long as you do your homework. I will share with you the basic knowledge you will need when buying bronze sculptures but I encourage you to further your knowledge by studying all that you can and learn from others in the field. The more you know the better you will be at determining the difference between a real bronze and a fake bronze, and more importantly the difference between a good buy and terrible buy.

How Is A Bronze Sculpture Made?

- The process begins with the art being sculpted into a material such as wood, clay, wax or other materials. Then a mold is made from the finished piece of art. This mold becomes the master for all of the sculptures made in that particular edition. Some sculptures require several molds depending on the complexities of that piece.

- The next step is to make a hollow wax "positive"duplicate of the artists original, at this point all the fine details are refined by the artisan to match the original sculpture.

- Next a funnel made of wax is added. This will be the entry point of the molten metal. There are also a series of wax gates (sprues) attached. This allows the bronze to flow in and air to flow out.

- It is then dipped into a ceramic solution many times to create several layers until a strong ceramic shell is formed.

- Then the ceramic mold is finished by placing into extremely high heat, this burns out any excess wax and strengthens the mold.

- The mold is now ready for the molten bronze to be poured. The content of a true fine art bronze is generally an alloy of 90% copper combined with silicone and manganese. These elements are poured into the ceramic mold, then after the bronze has solidified and cooled the mold is opened and the "raw" sculpture is exposed.

- From this point it cleansed of sand and any other particles, then the sculpture is assembled and a cleaning process referred to as metal chasing is performed, this addresses any imperfections that may have been left on the sculpture during the molding or shelling process.

- Finally the surface coloring (patina) is added to the finished bronze.

Identifying A Bronze Sculpture

Details

First look at the quality of the details in the face, hair, hands and feet areas of a human form; fur, paws, hooves and eyes in animal form sculptures. These are the hardest places to to get right in the casting. The quality or lack there of will be evident in these areas.

Patina

The finish on the sculpture (patina) should have rich colors with plenty of depth. Low quality sculptures often times have a dark patina because the thicker and darker the patina is, the more it can conceal the imperfections in the metal. Watch out for any chips, flakes or drips. These would not be evident on a true bronze sculpture.

Bases

Vintage bronze sculptures were rarely attached to a separate base especially non-bronze bases like marble. Watch out for bases that are shiny or new looking. Also watch out for bases that have metal tags with the artist name and title on them. There are virtually no original sculptures that have these types of tags. Also keep an eye out for bases that are identical on different sculptures, this is another example of a sculpture that was most likely mass produced.

Metal

Most reproduction "bronze" sculptures are really just cast iron with a false patina. Simply use a small magnet. If it sticks it is NOT bronze.

Signatures

Signatures and marks from the foundry are helpful for determining authenticity. Learning everything you can about these and how they should look are vital to your success.

Originals vs. Reproductions

Sculptures are widely available as reproductions by nearly every important artist complete with the artists signature. These sculptures are offered as "bronze" but the fact is, most are made of low quality materials that are assembled in China. These are mass produced and supplied to antique reproduction wholesalers and decorators. These sculptures are often mistaken as originals.

I recommend buying original sculptures that were cast by the artist themselves and have certification by a well established and respected appraiser. Do not take the buyers word for it.

Buying Bronze Sculptures

Most original sculptures that have been authenticated and appraised are found in fine art galleries, antique shops and auction houses. These are sculptures that already have an established provenance and usually have a high price tag.

There is not going to be much profit potential when buying from these establishments.

That is why I focus my search on garage sales, estate sales, thrift stores and flea markets. If you can identify a true bronze sculpture by using the steps I previously outlined, you just might discover a valuable sculpture for a cheap price. That's exactly what I did when I bought a D. H. Chiparus - "Dancing Indian" at an estate sale.

D. H. Chiparus - "Dancing Indian"

Bought for **$45** at Estate Sale

Sold for **$400** three weeks later.

Selling Bronze Sculptures

I have had the most luck selling my sculptures at high end auction houses and to private collectors. I also have had some success selling on Ebay. Another option if I'm looking to do a "quick flip" is to sell directly to dealers and gallery owners.

These are all effective ways to sell your sculptures. It is just a matter of personal preference and what works best for your business model.

Important Tips

Don't make a purchase decision based solely on signatures and or marks. There were many artists that had their own foundries and they never used marks. There are also sculptures with artist signatures that are reproductions.

Just because there is a C.O.A. (Certificates of Authenticity) that doesn't necessarily prove anything. They are not always a reliable and easily forged.

Watch out for sellers who claim that their reproduction is rare or has a high market value.

If you are comparing sculptures on the internet pay attention to the quality of the photos of the sculpture. If the photos are dark or the details are hard to see you can't be sure of what you will be receiving. On the other hand if there are a lot of close up photos showing the details, you can be pretty sure that they are confident of the quality of their sculpture. That being said I still highly recommend only buying sculptures in person that way you know exactly what you are getting.

Being at the right place at the right time means nothing if you are unprepared or unaware. - Rick Cheadle

Overview - Putting it all Together

I've given you a lot of information to digest. Make sure to take your time with it, and go back in case you haven't got it all. I can't stress enough how important it is to be thorough in all of these areas.

I wouldn't make a recommendation to you if it wasn't something I do myself. This overview will serve as a refresher, as well as a reference to guide your way through your daily actions.

Keep this overview handy, because you never know when you may need it.

Keep Your Risk Small and Your Profit Opportunity Big

The general rule is to never lose money. What this means is that if you do your due diligence before investing in any art, you may still lose money on that particular piece. Don't let that deter you from making massive profits.

Never invest more than you're willing to lose. This is a general mindset concept that will greatly affect your ability to make wise business decisions. You will always make more money when you start with where you're at and go at your own pace.

You've been given proven strategies that I use to make a lot of money over the long term. Though you may feel overwhelmed and a little intimidated by buying and selling art, as long as you start slow and follow my recommendations you should do great.

There is no telling where the next Picasso painting is going to show up. You won't know unless you try. My rule of thumb is to only buy art that I have authenticated, that is painted by a "listed" artists and has a verified auction record history.

Sharpen Your Skills

Study listed artists, examine their signatures and styles. Research completed auctions to see what sells and why. The more you know the better your art flipping prowess will become.

Become Familiar with How the Art Business Works and the Key Players

Know the ins and outs of how the art world operates. This will keep you in the game as a star player, rather than someone who sits on the sidelines. Your results will improve dramatically once you begin networking with all the right people.

Knowing Where to Find Desirable Art to Resell

Anywhere and everywhere. Always be on the hunt. I mostly focus on garage sales, estate sales and auctions but I have found valuable paintings in the garbage! Keep a sharp eye everywhere you go.

Authenticate, Authenticate, Authenticate!

Don't buy on a whim and do not buy with your heart. Be smart and go through all the recommended tips listed in chapter 5.

Decide where to sell your art

There are many options. The most bang for the buck will come from a major auction house. Private dealers, brokers, galleries and eBay are also great places to sell art.

An Example of How I Prospect Art

Let's say I happen to be driving down the street and see an Estate sale sign. I follow the signs to the house, park my car and before I get out I make sure I have my jeweler's loupe in my pocket. I also prepare my smart phone with web access on and the askart.com page is already loaded.

I walk in and look everything over. I spot a very cool still life painting and I can't quite make out the signature, so I pull out my jeweler's loupe and get a closer look. The signature reads 'L. Smith'.

I pull out my smart phone and enter "Smith" into askart.com search box. There are three listed artists with the name 'L. Smith', so I compare the signatures and there it is, a match! How exciting.

Now I have to make sure this painting is an actual painting and not a print. I hold the painting up to the light, and looking from the back of the painting I check for depth changes in the paint. The light shining through is uneven.

This is looking good, but let me check something else. I look through the loupe again at several areas around the canvas to make sure there are no dots which would indicate that this was a print. Good news.

No dots. It's looking very good but I still need to check something else. The dust cover on the back is partially ripped so I ask the estate sale folks if I can remove the rest of the cover. Then I begin to inspect further.

Upon removing the cover I see a gallery stamp from Chicago. Oh ya - I'm buying! Now to keep my poker face and negotiate a great price.

I have done this over and over and over again! There are a lot of people out there that just don't know what they have, and there are treasures everywhere. You just have to find them.

Resources

www.estatesales.net

www.auctionzip.com

garagesalefinder.com

www.askart.com

www.craigslist.org

fleaquest.com

www.ebay.com

www.liveauctioneers.com

www.shopgoodwill.com

www.artistssignatures.com

www.artnet.com

www.christies.com

gsaauctions.gov

rickcheadle.com

Conclusion

The strategies I covered in this book are the ones that work for me. All of the tools I have recommended are the actual tools that I have personally used. But that doesn't necessarily mean that they are the only tools out there. During your research you may find other resources to help you along the way. You literally can't learn enough about fine art buying and selling. That is why this business is so fun and exciting!

What this book covered is my buying and selling formula that delivers consistent results for me and they will work for you too, but only when you do the work and apply them correctly. Art flipping can be a lot of work but it is also a lot of fun and the rewards are so worth it!

I hope this book pumped you up and got you prepared to go out there and find your treasure! The next step is to put all of the information in this book to work and get out there and do it. It can literally change your life. I hope it does!

If you've enjoyed this book and think that the information is valuable, please head over to Amazon, take the time to share your thoughts, and post a review.

I would greatly appreciate it!

Thank you and Happy Treasure Hunting!

Rick Cheadle

www.rickcheadle.com

Printed in Great Britain
by Amazon